Sometimes at first sight the seashore can seem desolate and devoid of life, but if you look closely you will find that it is teeming with a myriad of strange creatures, and plants that can be seen nowhere else. This book will help you to find and recognise many of them.

First Edition

© LADYBIRD BOOKS LTD MCMLXXXI

Seaside Notebook

written by Pamela K Whitehead

photographs by Michael M Whitehead

Ladybird Books Loughborough

Introduction

The seashore is home for thousands of strange and beautiful creatures, although many are so small that you will not be able to see them unless you use a magnifying glass or a microscope. The larger creatures are for the most part easy to find once you know where to look, and the areas immediately surrounding the seashore, the cliffs and coastal plains will, too, provide you with a view of plants and birds specially adapted to their life alongside that most hostile yet productive of all environments, the sea. Apparently lifeless stretches of beach hold beneath the surface a host of unimaginable life forms and in the still pools left at low tide, under the rocks or hiding in the seaweed, quite different species flourish.

All the life of the seashore depends in some way on, or is affected by, the tides and, for instance, many creatures would die if not covered by water at least once a day. Yet they could not live in the deep oceans. Others can stand dry conditions for long periods and, therefore, are normally found on the uppermost limit of the shore at the highest point the water can reach. Yet others live close to the low tide line and can be out of the sea only for a very short time.

Each creature has its own particular zone on the shore. As you find them, therefore, always put them back safely in the area you found them because they cannot survive elsewhere.

Tides

The seashore, coastline and its life are all in some way affected by the rise and fall of the water, which we call tides. In general terms these are caused by the magnetic pull of the sun and moon on the earth. Although tides are regular, the height of the water may vary. There are very high tides, called spring tides, which are nothing to do with the season, and happen when the moon and the sun are in line with each other, thereby exerting more pull on the water. There are also very low, or neap tides. These occur when the sun and the moon are in opposition and pulling against each other.

Low tide and high tide in the same harbour

Rocks
Metamorphic rock

The many kinds of rocks to be seen along the coastline can be divided into three different types. The first we call igneous *rock* which started as molten lava, cooled and became hard. An example of this would be granite. The second sort of rock, which we call sedimentary, was built up over millions of years from layers of rock particles or the remains of sea creatures. Chalk and limestone were formed in this manner. Thirdly we have rocks such as slate which, because of great changes in temperature and sometimes enormous pressure, have been altered in structure. These we call metamorphic *rocks*.

Erosion

The incoming tide is rather like a huge battering ram. Tonnes of water carrying hundreds of small pebbles, larger boulders and churned up sand are smashed against the land. Bit by bit the rocks are worn down and cliffs crumble. Wind and weather also attack the coastline. Rain washes away the softer rock while frost and ice can crack the hardest surface. This we call erosion, and its effects can be seen in the arches, stacks and rocky islands dotted around our shores.

Over many years large areas which were once part of mainland Britain, including whole villages and even forests, have been engulfed by the waves. To prevent erosion today many areas along the coastline have special defences to keep the sea at bay.

Sedimentary rock

9

Sand

Although erosion means that every day small pieces of land slip into the sea, without it we would not have sandy beaches. Huge rocks are broken down into smooth pebbles which are pounded together by the sea until they become smaller and smaller, finally turning into coarse fragments of sand. The finest sand around the coastline is made up of the crushed remains and shells of millions of sea creatures. In a way, sand washed on to the beach prevents further erosion as the shoreline grows higher and becomes in time a natural barrier formed between the land and the sea.

Dunes and Marram

In some parts of the country you will see places where the sand has been built up to such an extent that it has formed hills, called dunes, sometimes stretching far inland. The loose grains of sand are blown by the wind and are always on the move until plants such as Marram Grass take hold. This plant has very long roots which are able to dig deeply into the sand. In doing this they also anchor the sand in one place. As time goes on Marram Grass creates small areas of soil in which other plants can grow.

Sea Bindweed

Between June and September you will find the pink and white striped flowers of the Sea Bindweed growing along the coast. It can often be seen decorating cliff tops where taller, less hardy plants cannot live. Sea Bindweed survives in the poorest of soil, and as it lies very low on the ground it is not damaged by strong winds. Because it can grow in such conditions, it is one of the first plants to follow Marram Grass on to the dunes, where its creeping roots ensure it a firm grip on the sand.

Scarlet Pimpernel

The Scarlet Pimpernel is found everywhere, in fields, waste places and on cultivated ground where it is a stubborn weed and the despair of gardeners. On the dunes, however, it attains a particular importance in helping to bind the sand with its spreading, carpet-like growth. You will sometimes find pink or blue varieties of this flower, but it was in its familiar scarlet colouring that it achieved fame in Baroness Orczy's books. These were about a man who called himself the Scarlet Pimpernel and used the red flower as his signature.

Seaside Centaury

One of our prettiest flowers is the Seaside Centaury, which can be seen at the coast between June and September. This plant favours areas which are sheltered from the wind as, unlike the Sea Bindweed and Scarlet Pimpernel, it does not hug the ground closely but grows erect. Its pink-purple flowers are so distinctive that you can easily identify it, although it can be confused with its close cousin, the Common Centaury, which grows both inland and at the seaside.

Marsh Helleborine

Many orchids are to be found growing in soils which are rich in lime. It seems at first odd to think of them in connection with the seaside until you remember that sand is the ground remains of rocks and shells, and limestone is formed from this type of material. The Marsh Helleborine, which is a member of the orchid family, can be found growing in the wet areas between sand dunes which are known as slacks. You can also see it in marshes and fens. Look out for the crimson, white and brown flowers growing in groups in July and August.

Lichens

Lichens are a mixture of two plants living together, a fungus and a very simple green plant called an alga. Because they like to grow where the air is clean, the coast is a very good place to see them, and you will even find Lichens in areas where they are splashed by the high tide. Indeed, as you look at some cliffs and large rocks you can see how far up the tide line goes. Where the water reaches to will be bare or barnacle covered, whilst above it you will see Lichens and other plants growing.

Few Lichens have common names. This one is Xanthoria parientina

16

Kelp

Unlike the plants of the land, seaweeds do not have roots and are in fact algae. They may look as if they are growing out of the rocks but the tough, root-like structure you can see is there only to anchor them down. This holdfast, therefore, is not a means of obtaining food, as with the roots of land plants, but seaweeds share with land plants the ability to obtain energy from sunlight using a substance called chlorophyll which is contained in their fronds. Some seaweeds known as Kelps can only be seen when there is a very low tide. These are the very large, brown coloured seaweeds that are sometimes washed up on the beach after heavy gales.

Bladder Wrack

The brown-green seaweed known as Bladder Wrack is easy to study because it is often attached to rocks close to the shore. The small bubbles on the fronds are called bladders and are filled with air, thus enabling the seaweed to float towards the surface of the water. This means that it is able to absorb a lot of sunlight to make energy. All seaweeds provide food and shelter for hundreds of creatures. The Flat Periwinkle is often to be found on the Bladder Wrack, its round shape and colour making it look like another bladder. Can you see the Flat Periwinkles in the picture?

Periwinkle

Wherever seaweed is to be found on the shore, there too will be the Periwinkles, for algal seaweed forms the food of this family. Among them will be the brown, black and red Edible Periwinkle which lives on and under rocks in the wetter areas. This is the winkle which is sold in kiosks along the sea front. Some species of Periwinkles can live at the high tide line and have developed lungs to help them to cope with the long periods spent out of water. Others which are out of the sea less often breathe through gills.

Barnacles

Barnacles, seen at low tide as they cling to rocks, sea walls or cliff faces, appear to be lifeless. As the tide covers them, however, they begin to feed. An opening appears in the top of the greyish white plated shell and its small 'tongue' sieves the water for minute particles of food. In fact this is not the mouth at all, but the remains of what used to be legs! When attaching itself to a permanent resting place the Barnacle does so by cementing its head to the surface first. For the rest of its life it will remain in exactly the same position, never moving again.

Limpets

Close to the Barnacles you will usually find the larger shells of Limpets, which are a type of sea-snail. Unlike other snails the Limpet cannot withdraw into its shell for protection but relies on attaching itself very firmly to the rock by means of a sucker foot. Thus its soft underside is safe, leaving only the hard outer shell exposed to potential enemies. If you try to prise a Limpet from its rock, you will know just how powerful the sucker foot is! When covered by water the Limpet moves around grazing on green algae, but as the tide retreats it returns to exactly the same spot each day.

Dog Whelk *opposite*

The Dog Whelk is very common on rocks amongst Barnacles and Mussels, for it feeds on other shelled creatures. The Barnacle, for instance, which takes all the pounding the sea can offer, has little defence against this snail which can pierce its hard plates and eat the soft inner body. The shell colour of the Dog Whelk is related to the food it eats. This explains why you will see dark or even striped varieties as well as the pale colour of the Barnacle feeders.

Mussels *below right*

Close to the water at low tide, along some areas of the coast, you may come across hundreds of dark blue shells packed tightly together on the rocks. These will be Mussels. When very young, Mussels move about the sea-bed, but when they find a suitable rock they attach themselves to it using short threads, secreted by the foot, known as byssus. If you look closely you will see the byssus for yourself. Should the Mussel break away from the rock it can produce the threads again when it finds another resting place. A tiny crab called the Pea Crab makes its home inside the shell of the Mussel.

Dog Whelk

Mussel

Chiton

The Chiton has another very interesting name, the Coat of Mail Shell. Like the ancient armour it is named after, the Chiton is made up of many separate plates which are all joined together yet flexible. You will find this creature browsing on algae on the underside of rocks, to which it clings very firmly. It looks rather like the familiar woodlice you will find in the garden, and like them the Chiton is able to curl tightly into a ball when disturbed.

Chiton

Cushion Star *opposite below*

A close relative of the Starfish is the Cushion Star, which is a creature of the south and west coasts of Britain where it makes its home under rocks. If you compare the two you will see how different they are, for the Cushion Star is far more rounded and does not have distinct arms. It does, however, have suckers on the underside of the rays which help it to move around the rocks, just as a Starfish has. If you turn one over on to its back you will see how quickly it rights itself again.

Starfish

If you should find Mussels as you explore the rocks, look carefully, because they are a source of food for Starfish which will probably be there too. They are easy to recognise because they have distinct arms, or rays, usually five, but some species have more. Starfish are very odd creatures because they have no head, but each arm has an eye at its tip and its mouth is on the underside of the central disc. The arms are equipped with suckers which enable Starfish to cling firmly to rocks and shells, and if an arm is lost it will grow again.

Starfish

Cushion Star

25

Brittle Star

Brittle Stars are small and easily missed. If you look carefully, however, you will find them clinging to the underside of rocks. Their five long, thin arms are very fragile and will break off easily, although they do grow again. Some species burrow into the sand, leaving one arm above the surface to ensure a supply of oxygen, which is taken from the water. The arms are also used for feeding and to help the Brittle Star move around.

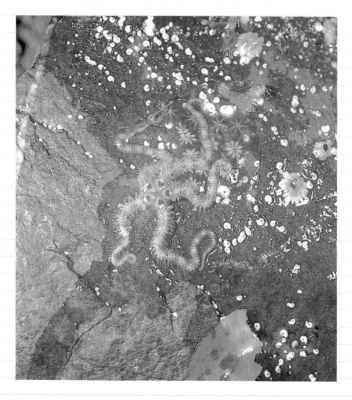

Sea Urchin

Despite their round, spiny shape, Sea Urchins are often very difficult to find because they hide themselves so well. One species even covers itself with pieces of seaweed and debris. They are very pretty and several kinds are edible. When an Urchin is stripped of its spines and cleaned, the shell (called a test) which surrounds the soft body can be seen. Underwater, long tube feet appear outside the body and the Sea Urchin uses these and its spines to move around the sea floor. You can sometimes find the tests washed up on the beach.

Sand Dollar

Closely related to the Sea Urchins is a group of animals known as Sand Dollars. The one shown is called the Sea Potato. They spend their lives buried in the sand which they eat and obtain food from. The feet are long tubes which extend from the test and between the spines. The exits form petal-like shapes of holes which can be seen on the dead test. Apart from digging in the sand at the lowest limit of the tide, the best time to find Sand Dollars is after storms which churn up the sand and often deposit these creatures, sometimes in great numbers, along the shoreline.

Rock Dwellers

Marine worms come in many different shapes and forms, ranging from very simple structures to highly complex specialised organisms. Some of them actually burrow into rocks, whilst others live in sand and mud filled crevices. The burrows of the two worms can be clearly seen in the picture. Some other creatures also bore into rocks, like the Piddock, which is a shelled animal, and a species of Sea Urchin.

A relative of the Piddock, the Shipworm, bores not into rock but into wood and is known to have caused the sinking of many wooden hulled ships, one of the most famous being Sir Francis Drake's Golden Hind.

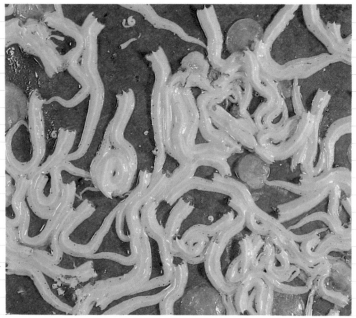

Tube Dwellers

We usually think of shells in connection with animals such as Periwinkles and Mussels, which group is known collectively as molluscs, but there are several species of worm that construct hard tubular shells. You will find them on the underside of rocks and stones, often in great masses. They feed and breathe through dozens of hairy tentacles which filter microscopic particles of food and oxygen from the water. When disturbed or at low tide, these worms can withdraw completely into their tubes and close the entrances securely with specially adapted limbs that work rather like a plug.

Sand Mason

You will not have to scramble over the rocks to find the knobbly, ragged topped homes of the Sand Masons. They can be seen quite easily, sometimes in their hundreds, on the wet shoreline in the sheltered sandy bays that this worm prefers. Bit by bit the Sand Mason sticks together grains of sand, making a hollow tube which can stretch as far as 30 centimetres under the surface. You will probably never see the worm itself, because by the time you have dug up all the tube it will have long since wriggled out of the other end and hidden itself in the sand.

Lug Worm

If you want to find Lug Worms you will have to dig for them, because these creatures live in the sand and mud. It is easy to discover where they are by walking along the wet beach at low tide. Dotted about you will see small, oddly shaped piles of sand. These are called worm casts, and the Lug Worms will be underneath. Worm casts are formed from the sand which has been eaten by the Lug Worms. They extract food particles from the sand and then push the unwanted material up to the surface.

Lug Worm casts

Rag Worm

It is a little more difficult to find the brightly coloured Rag Worms, because they move about in search of food. You will find some types in amongst the rocks and seaweed towards the edge of the water. Others burrow into the mud and slime at the bottom of harbours and estuaries. Still another variety makes its home with the Hermit Crab, in its shell! The largest member of this family is the King Rag which can grow up to 40 centimetres long and is as thick as a finger.

33

Beadlet Anemone

Anemones are amongst the prettiest animals to be seen in rock pools. They have no skeletons and their soft jewel coloured bodies are usually stuck very firmly to rocks. This one is the Beadlet, so called because of the ring of blue dots around its mouth. When it is covered by water, stinging tentacles – about two hundred of them – sift the sea for food. When caught the food is swiftly transferred into the mouth and the tentacles withdraw until the Anemone has eaten its meal. The tentacles only emerge in water, so all you will see of the animal on dry rocks is a jelly-like blob of red, green or strawberry colours.

Opelet Anemone

Another common Anemone is the purple-brown or pale green Opelet, which is also called Snakelocks. It is much larger than the Beadlet, althouth it has the same number of tentacles. If you watch for a time you may see this Anemone moving slowly around the rock pool. It does this by swelling its base with water until it extends forward like a foot. Unlike the Beadlet, the Opelet cannot close itself. If it becomes stranded out of water at low tide it collapses into a soggy mess on the rock and is not recognisable as an Anemone at all.

Breadcrumb Sponge

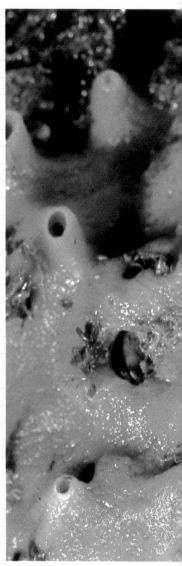

Although they look like plants, Sponges are in fact very simple animals. This one is called the Breadcrumb Sponge and you will see it in colours of white, orange or brown, as well as green. Like the Barnacles, Sponges are not able to move, and they obtain their food from the sea which covers them most of the time. Each day many litres of water are absorbed, then expelled after food has been extracted. Other smaller animals take advantage of the protection offered by Sponges and spend their lives in the holes in the soft mass. You will sometimes find the Breadcrumb Sponge covering large areas of rocks close to the low tide line.

Hermit Crabs sometimes use pieces of sponge to camouflage their shells

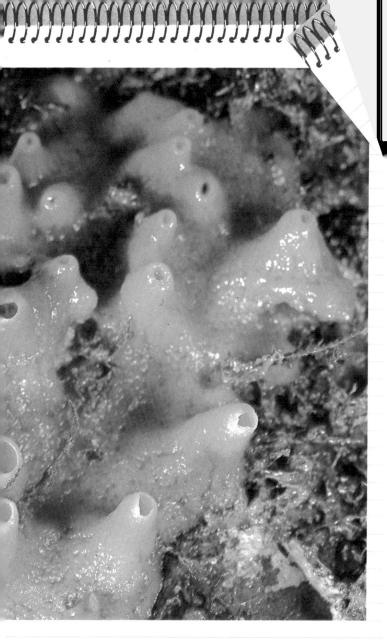

Shore Crab

The Shore Crab is usually to be found in shallow water, but it likes a wide variety of areas and you will see it in rock pools and harbours, sometimes right up to the high tide limit. The usual size of the Shore Crab is 3–4 centimetres, although they often grow much larger. Crabs have their hard skeleton on the outside of their bodies, the soft fleshy parts being inside. This means that every so often a Crab must shed its outer skeleton as it grows in size. When this happens the Crab is at the mercy of its enemies as the new shell is quite soft for a number of hours.

Hairy Crab *opposite*

You will know how this Crab got its name as soon as you see it, for its red-brown body is indeed very hairy. This is another method by which Crabs avoid being seen by their enemies – or even by you as you turn over the stones in the wet areas where they hide. The body of the Hairy Crab does not grow to a large size, only to about 2 centimetres, but as you can see it has one enormous claw which looks far too big for the rest of its body.

Velvet Swimming Crab

The Velvet Swimming Crab is interesting because its rear legs are in the shape of oars. This means that it is a very strong swimmer. You will find it hiding under rocks at low tide. The Velvet Swimming Crab is very colourful and can grow up to 8 centimetres in length − but beware, it will certainly nip you if you do not handle it carefully. Like the other members of the Crab family, it is a scavenger and feeds on dead fish or other sea animals. The longer claws are used both for defence and to tear larger pieces of food apart and direct them into its mouth.

Hermit Crab

If you see a shell moving at great speed over the sandy bottom of a rock pool, you can be certain that it contains a Hermit Crab. This creature has a hard outer skeleton over part of its body, just like other Crabs, but it also has a soft tail end. It therefore spends its life inside empty shells of sea snails, like the Whelk and Periwinkle, where it is protected. It must find a new home from time to time as its body grows, and it is only then that the Hermit Crab exposes itself completely, and only for the shortest time possible.

Edible Crab

Although the very big Edible Crabs are only found in deep water, you will see smaller ones in amongst rocks on the shoreline. The colours are pink or brown – the deep red you see in the shops only happens when the Crab is cooked. The young Edible Crab will play dead if frightened, unlike the adults which are more likely to try and nip you with their huge black pincers.

Masked Crab

Crabs are able to escape their enemies because they are strong and well protected enough to defend themselves, or their colouring makes them difficult to see, or because they hide themselves under rocks. The Masked Crab is a little different because it spends its life buried in the wet sand in shallow water. To enable it to live, nature has equipped it with very long antennae which join together to form a hollow tube. Part of this remains on the surface when the Masked Crab is buried in the sand, and this means that it is able to breathe by drawing water down to its gills through the tube.

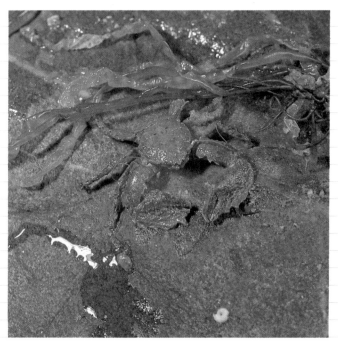

Porcelain Crab

Although it looks very much like a Crab, this animal is more closely related to the Lobster. Most of its time is spent hiding away under rocks and stones, or in mud and gravel, for which its flat body is well adapted. You will find large numbers sheltering together, particularly in rock crevices, during low tide. Their colouring blends very well with the background, and when frightened they pull their legs and claws tightly into the sides of their bodies so that they look a different shape. This defence helps them remain unnoticed when they are exposed.

Squat Lobster

While exploring the rock pools you may come across what looks like an oddly shaped Crab. If it has an oval rather than a round body, very long front legs and antennae, you are probably looking at a Squat Lobster. Usually it is tucked away beneath rocks with only its long claws visible. By flapping its tail against its body the Squat Lobster can move and swim very quickly, as you will discover if you try to pick one up. The colours may be brown, red or orange, and some species can grow up to 15 centimetres long.

Prawns

If you want to find very large Prawns, you will have to go out to the lowest limit of the tide and search in the rock pools and amongst the seaweed there. You may be surprised at the colours you find, for like the Edible Crab, most Prawns only become the bright red colour you see in the shops after they have been cooked. Some of them are transparent, making them even more difficult to find, while another species protects itself by changing colour according to the seaweed it is hiding in, or even whether it is day or night.

Blennies

The shallow coastal waters are home for many types of fish, some of which are able to live within the areas between the tides. Among them are the Blennies, which are interesting because the pelvic fins are adapted to form leg-like structures on which the fish can prop itself when resting. You can see also that the eyes are placed high on its head, enabling the Blenny to clearly sight its prey. It is a voracious feeder, the inside of its jaw being lined with rows of small sharp teeth. The colours of this fish, normally browns, greys and greens, become brighter when it is excited, and certain changes in colour take place during the breeding season.

Scorpion Fish

With its big, flat head and covering of sharp spines, the Scorpion Fish is a very odd looking creature. Like most of the shoreline fish it can live if necessary in very little water, and at low tide you will sometimes find it hiding in wet gravel under rocks, or even buried in the sand. Its mottled brown, grey and white colouring makes it very hard to see, especially as it does not move very often, even in water, preferring to spend long periods lying still at the bottom of rock pools.

Sand Eel

Sand Eels swim in large shoals, preferring the shallower water of sandy bays. When the tide goes out many of them burrow for safety into the sand, sliding easily under the surface with the help of their long pointed jaws. You can sometimes spot small holes in the wet sand close to the low tide mark. The Sand Eels will be beneath and they are easy to remove and study, although they will wriggle furiously when disturbed.

Herring Gull

Screaming and squabbling, the Herring Gulls let you know that you have reached the coast. These big white birds are a common sight all round our shores, and wherever there are high cliffs they nest in great numbers. They are called Herring Gulls because flocks of the birds used to follow the herring fleets from port and escort them back into land, ever hopeful of rich pickings from discarded fish. They are not fussy eaters, however, and you will see them raiding rubbish tips and coming down to feed on scraps thrown by people along the sea front.

Kittiwake

Flying amongst the Herring Gulls you may see the smaller, more delicately formed Kittiwakes. They are much shyer than their bold relatives and you will probably not be able to get close to them. When feeding they hover over the water before swooping down to snatch up a titbit. If you listen to the Kittiwake's call you will discover how it got its name because the bird sounds as if it is crying 'kittiwake'.

When things go wrong
Guillemot *facing page*

When oil tankers have accidents at sea and spill their cargoes into the water, it does not just mean dirty beaches on which you cannot play. To many thousands of sea creatures the oil is fatal. Animals which survive the pollution may find that it has killed their food supply, so they die *themselves. Sea birds like the Guillemot that land on the water become covered in the oil. It sticks their feathers together so they cannot fly or swim. When the bird tries to clean itself it eats the oil and is poisoned.*

INDEX